EVERYTHING TOKEN

Navigating the World of Cryptocurrency Tokens

CHAPTER ONE

CHAPTER TWO

CHAPTER THREE

CHAPTER FOUR

CHAPTER FIVE

Token Launch Mechanisms

Initial Coin Offerings (ICOs)

Security Token Offerings (STOs)

Initial Decentralized Exchange Offerings (IDOs)

Initial Exchange Offerings (IEOs)

CHAPTER SIX

Use Cases of Tokens

Decentralized Finance (DeFi)

Non-Fungible Tokens (NFTs)

Gaming and Virtual Assets

Supply Chain Management

Identity Verification and Digital Rights Management

CHAPTER SEVEN

Token Investment Strategies

Fundamental Analysis of Token Projects

Technical Analysis and Market Sentiment

Risk Management and Portfolio Diversification

CHAPTER EIGHT

Token Security and Best Practices

Smart Contract Audits

Wallet Security and Cold Storage

Avoiding Scams and Fraudulent Projects

CHAPTER NINE

CHAPTER TEN

Conclusion and Future Outlook

Summary of Key Concepts

Reflections on the Future of Tokenomics

Resources for Further Learning

INTRODUCTION
TO TOKENS

1. Definition and Characteristics of Tokens

In the rapidly evolving landscape of crypto currency and blockchain technology, tokens represent digital assets that are created, stored, and transferred on decentralized networks. They are programmable units of value that can serve various functions within blockchain ecosystems. Key characteristics of tokens include:

Programmability: Tokens can be programmed to execute specific functions, such as triggering smart contracts or facilitating automated transactions.

Fungibility: Many tokens are fungible, meaning that each unit is interchangeable with another unit of the same type and value, similar to traditional currencies.

Divisibility: Tokens can be divided into smaller units, allowing for micro transactions and precise value exchange.

Examples of tokens include utility tokens, which grant access to a product or service within a platform; security tokens, which represent ownership in a real-world asset; and governance tokens, which enable stakeholders to participate in decision-making processes within decentralized autonomous organizations

(DAOs).

2. Importance of Tokens in the Cryptocurrency Ecosystem

Tokens play a crucial role in the cryptocurrency ecosystem, serving as the backbone of decentralized applications (dApps), blockchain-based platforms, and digital economies. Their significance stems from several key factors:

Facilitating Transactions: Tokens enable peer-to-peer transactions and facilitate the exchange of value without the need for intermediaries, thereby reducing transaction costs and enhancing financial inclusion.

Incentivizing Participation: in many blockchain networks, tokens serve as incentives to encourage user participation, contribution, and engagement. Participants are rewarded with tokens for validating transactions, securing the network, or providing computational resources.

Enabling Smart Contracts: Tokens are integral to the functionality of smart contracts, self-executing agreements that automatically enforce predefined conditions when certain criteria are met. Smart contracts enable the automation of a wide range of processes, including escrow services, token sales, and supply chain management.

Driving Innovation: Tokens fuel innovation by providing a flexible and efficient means of crowdfunding, incentivizing research and development, and experimenting with new business models. They enable entrepreneurs and developers to monetize their ideas, tokenize real-world assets, and explore novel applications of blockchain technology.

Decentralizing Finance: Through decentralized finance (DeFi) platforms, tokens enable borderless lending, borrowing, trading, and investing without reliance on traditional financial intermediaries. DeFi has the potential to democratize access to financial services and reshape the global financial landscape.

In summary, tokens represent a fundamental building block of the cryptocurrency ecosystem, facilitating trustless transactions, incentivizing network participation, and driving innovation across various industries and sectors.

This detailed breakdown provides a comprehensive overview of the introduction to tokens chapter, laying the groundwork for readers to understand the significance and implications of tokens in the context of crypto currency and blockchain technology.

CHAPTER TWO
TYPES OF TOKENS

1. Utility Tokens

Utility tokens are digital assets that provide access to a specific product, service, or platform within a blockchain ecosystem. They are designed to serve a practical purpose and are often used to facilitate transactions or access features within decentralized applications (dApps).

Definition and Characteristics of Utility Tokens:

Utility tokens represent the right to use a product or service and do not inherently represent ownership or equity in the issuing company.

They are typically built on blockchain platforms such as Ethereum and utilize smart contracts to automate token functionality.

Utility tokens may have various functions, including access to premium features, voting rights, or discounts on services within the associated platform.

How Utility Tokens Function Within Blockchain Ecosystems:

Utility tokens act as a means of incentivizing user engagement and participation within decentralized networks.

Users acquire utility tokens through purchases, contributions to token sales (e.g., Initial Coin Offerings), or as rewards for contributing value to the ecosystem (e.g., mining or staking).

Once acquired, utility tokens can be used to access platform services, pay for transactions, or participate in governance processes.

Examples of Popular Utility Tokens and Their Use Cases:

Ethereum (ETH): ETH serves as the native cryptocurrency of the Ethereum blockchain and is used to pay for transaction fees, deploy smart contracts, and interact with dApps.

Binance Coin (BNB): BNB is the native utility token of the Binance cryptocurrency exchange and provides users with discounts on trading fees, participation in token sales, and access to premium features.

Uniswap (UNI): UNI is the governance and utility token of the Uniswap decentralized exchange (DEX), allowing users to participate in protocol governance and earn rewards for providing liquidity to trading pools.

Chainlink (LINK): LINK is used to pay for data feeds and services within the Chainlink decentralized oracle network, enabling smart contracts to securely interact with real-world data sources.

Utility tokens span a wide range of industries and applications, including decentralized finance (DeFi), gaming, supply chain management, and identity verification. They play a vital role in driving user adoption, incentivizing network participation, and fostering innovation within the blockchain ecosystem.

2. Security Tokens

Security tokens represent ownership or investment in a real-world asset and are subject to securities regulations in many jurisdictions. They offer investors various rights, including ownership stakes, profit-sharing opportunities, or voting rights within the issuing entity.

Understanding Security Tokens and Their Regulatory Framework:

Security tokens are digital representations of traditional securities, such as stocks, bonds, or real estate holdings, issued on a blockchain.

They are subject to securities laws and regulations, which vary by jurisdiction and often require compliance with registration, disclosure, and investor protection requirements.

The regulatory framework for security tokens aims to safeguard investor interests, ensure market transparency, and prevent fraudulent activities.

Key Characteristics of Security Tokens, Including Ownership and Profit-Sharing Rights:

Security tokens typically represent ownership or equity in the underlying asset or company issuing the tokens.

Holders of security tokens may be entitled to dividends, profit distributions, or voting rights proportional to their token holdings.

Security tokens may offer additional benefits such as asset-backed security, fractional ownership, or liquidity through secondary trading markets.

Compliance Considerations for Issuing and Trading Security Tokens:

Issuers of security tokens must adhere to applicable securities regulations, which may involve filing prospectuses, obtaining regulatory approvals, and conducting investor accreditation checks.

Platforms facilitating the issuance or trading of security tokens must comply with know-your-customer (KYC) and anti-money laundering (AML) regulations to prevent illicit activities and ensure investor protection.

Secondary trading of security tokens is subject to regulatory oversight, including trading venue registration, transaction reporting, and investor suitability assessments.

Security tokens offer several advantages over traditional

securities, including increased liquidity, fractional ownership opportunities, and reduced transaction costs. However, navigating the regulatory landscape and ensuring compliance with securities laws are critical considerations for issuers and investors alike.

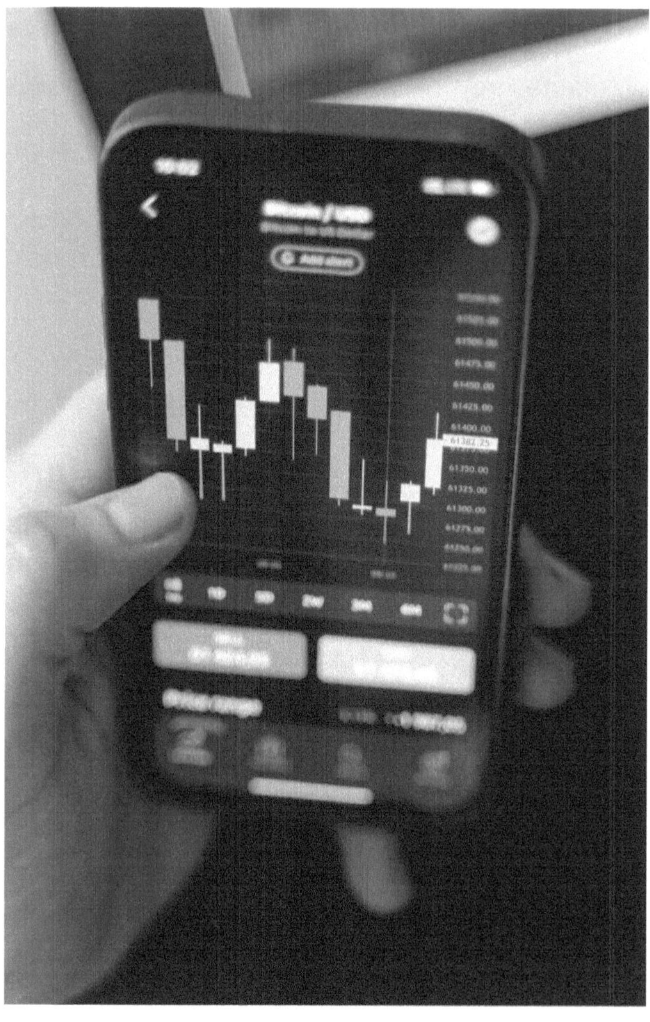

3. Governance Tokens

Governance tokens are cryptographic tokens that enable stakeholders to participate in the decision-making processes of decentralized autonomous organizations (DAOs) and other decentralized protocols. They empower token holders to propose and vote on changes to the network's parameters, protocols, and governance structures.

Exploring the Role of Governance Tokens in Decentralized Autonomous Organizations (DAOs):

Governance tokens serve as the mechanism through which decentralized communities govern and manage their protocols.

In DAOs, governance tokens represent voting power, allowing holders to propose, debate, and vote on proposals related to network upgrades, fund allocation, and protocol changes.

Governance tokens align the interests of token holders with the long-term sustainability and development of the decentralized ecosystem.

How Governance Tokens Enable Stakeholder Participation and Decision-Making:

Governance tokens grant holders the right to participate in governance processes by staking or delegating their tokens to vote on proposals.

Token holders can submit governance proposals, discuss them within the community, and cast votes according to their token holdings.

The voting outcomes determine whether proposed changes are implemented, providing a decentralized mechanism for community-driven decision-making.

Case Studies of Successful Governance Token Models:

Compound (COMP): Compound's governance token, COMP, enables token holders to vote on changes to the protocol, including adjustments to interest rates, collateral factors, and supported assets.

Uniswap (UNI): UNI, the governance token of Uniswap, grants holders voting power over protocol upgrades, fee structures, and the allocation of community treasury funds.

MakerDAO (MKR): MKR token holders govern the MakerDAO protocol, which maintains the stability of the DAI stablecoin by adjusting parameters such as the stability fee and collateral types.

Governance tokens are instrumental in fostering community engagement, ensuring transparency, and decentralizing decision-making within blockchain networks. They empower stakeholders to collectively shape the direction and governance of decentralized protocols, driving innovation and resilience in the decentralized ecosystem.

4. Non-Fungible Tokens (NFTs)

Non-fungible tokens (NFTs) are unique digital assets that represent ownership or proof of authenticity of a specific item or piece of content. Unlike fungible tokens, each NFT is distinct and cannot be exchanged on a one-to-one basis.

Definition and Characteristics of Non-Fungible Tokens:

NFTs are indivisible digital assets that exist on blockchain networks, typically conforming to standards such as ERC-721 or ERC-1155.

Each NFT contains metadata that defines its unique attributes, provenance, and ownership history, making it distinguishable from other tokens.

NFTs are interoperable across different platforms and can represent a wide range of digital and physical assets, including art, music, videos, virtual real estate, and in-game items.

Use Cases of NFTs in Digital Art, Gaming, Collectibles, and Intellectual Property:

Digital Art: NFTs revolutionize the art world by enabling artists to tokenize their creations, prove ownership, and monetize digital artwork through token sales and auctions.

Gaming: NFTs introduce ownership and scarcity to in-game assets, allowing players to buy, sell, and trade unique items across different gaming platforms.

Collectibles: NFTs enable the creation of digital collectibles, such as trading cards, virtual pets, and limited-edition merchandise, fostering a vibrant market for digital ownership.

Intellectual Property: NFTs provide a secure and transparent means of representing ownership rights, licensing agreements, and royalties for digital content creators, authors, and musicians.

Challenges and Opportunities Associated with NFT Adoption:

Scalability and Interoperability: The growing demand for NFTs poses challenges related to blockchain scalability, transaction costs, and interoperability across different platforms.

Regulatory Considerations: NFTs raise legal and regulatory questions regarding copyright, intellectual property rights, and the enforceability of digital contracts.

Market Speculation and Sustainability: The NFT market is

susceptible to speculative bubbles and market volatility, necessitating responsible investment practices and sustainable business models.

Despite these challenges, NFTs present numerous opportunities for innovation, creativity, and economic empowerment. They democratize access to digital ownership, redefine the concept of value in the digital age, and create new avenues for artists, creators, and collectors to monetize and showcase their work.

Non-Fungible Tokens (NFTs) are unique digital assets that represent ownership or proof of authenticity of a specific item or piece of content. Unlike fungible tokens, each NFT is distinct and cannot be exchanged on a one-to-one basis.

Here are some key characteristics and aspects of NFTs:

Indivisibility: Each NFT is indivisible, meaning it cannot be split into smaller units like cryptocurrencies such as Bitcoin or Ethereum.

Metadata: NFTs contain metadata that defines their unique attributes, provenance, and ownership history. This metadata can include information such as the creator's name, creation date, and any additional details about the item represented by the NFT.

Interoperability: NFTs are interoperable across different platforms and can represent a wide range of digital and physical assets, including art, music, videos, virtual real estate, and in-game items.

Token Standards: NFTs on blockchain networks often conform to standards such as ERC-721 or ERC-1155 (Ethereum Request for Comments), which provide guidelines for the creation and management of non-fungible tokens.

Ownership and Proof of Authenticity: NFTs serve as a digital certificate of ownership and proof of authenticity for the associated item or content. The blockchain ledger records the ownership and transaction history of each NFT, ensuring transparency and immutability.

NFTs have gained significant popularity in various industries, including:

Digital Art: NFTs have revolutionized the art world by enabling artists to tokenize their creations, prove ownership, and monetize digital artwork through token sales and auctions.

Gaming: NFTs introduce ownership and scarcity to in-game assets, allowing players to buy, sell, and trade unique items across different gaming platforms.

Collectibles: NFTs enable the creation of digital collectibles, such as trading cards, virtual pets, and limited-edition merchandise, fostering a vibrant market for digital ownership.

Intellectual Property: NFTs provide a secure and transparent means of representing ownership rights, licensing agreements, and royalties for digital content creators, authors, and musicians.

Despite the opportunities presented by NFTs, there are also challenges to consider, including scalability and interoperability issues, regulatory considerations, and market speculation.

Overall, NFTs represent a transformative technology that democratizes access to digital ownership, redefines the concept of value in the digital age, and creates new avenues for artists, creators, and collectors to monetize and showcase their work.

CHAPTER THREE: TOKEN STANDARDS

1. ERC-20 Token Standard:

The ERC-20 token standard stands as one of the most prevalent and foundational standards for creating fungible tokens on the Ethereum blockchain. Introduced by Ethereum Improvement Proposal (EIP) 20, ERC-20 tokens adhere to specific functions and interfaces, enabling interoperability among different Ethereum-based projects. Key features of ERC-20 tokens include their transferability, divisibility, and compatibility with various Ethereum wallets and decentralized exchanges. These tokens find widespread use across a variety of applications, including utility tokens for decentralized applications (DApps), stablecoins pegged to fiat currencies, and security tokens representing ownership in real-world assets. The ERC-20 standard has played a pivotal role in fueling the growth of the Ethereum token ecosystem, facilitating tokenization and innovation in decentralized finance (DeFi), gaming, and digital assets.

2. ERC-721 Token Standard:

In contrast to ERC-20 tokens, the ERC-721 token standard serves as the foundation for creating non-fungible tokens (NFTs) on the Ethereum blockchain. ERC-721 tokens are unique digital assets that represent ownership of distinct items, such as digital art, collectibles, virtual real estate, and in-game assets. Each ERC-721 token possesses a unique identifier and can be transferred or traded among users, enabling digital scarcity and provable ownership on the blockchain. The ERC-721 standard has sparked a revolution in the digital collectibles space, spawning vibrant marketplaces, innovative projects, and new forms of digital expression. NFTs built on the ERC-721 standard have gained mainstream attention, attracting artists, creators, and investors seeking to participate in the burgeoning NFT market.

3. Other Token Standards and Protocols:

Beyond ERC-20 and ERC-721, the tokenization landscape encompasses a diverse array of standards and protocols catering to various use cases and requirements. These include standards like ERC-1155, which combines the functionality of both ERC-20 and ERC-721, allowing for the creation of fungible, semi-fungible, and non-fungible tokens within a single contract. Additionally, blockchain platforms like Binance Smart Chain (BEP-20) and TRON (TRC-20) have introduced their own token standards, providing alternatives for developers and users seeking interoperability and scalability. Moreover, emerging standards focus on interoperability and cross-chain functionality, enabling seamless token transfer and communication across different blockchain networks. Industry-specific standards tailored for decentralized applications, governance mechanisms, and regulatory compliance further contribute to the evolving tokenization landscape, offering new possibilities for innovation and collaboration in the blockchain industry.

This chapter provides readers with a comprehensive overview of token standards, emphasizing the significance of ERC-20, ERC-721, and other protocols shaping the tokenization ecosystem. It explores the features, use cases, and implications of these standards, highlighting their role in driving innovation and adoption across various industries. Let me know if you need further clarification or if there are any additional details you'd like to incorporate!

CHAPTER THREE: TOKENOMICS FUNDAMENTALS

1. Token Supply and Distribution:

Token supply and distribution refer to the total number of tokens issued and how they are allocated among various stakeholders within a blockchain ecosystem. Key points include:

Token Creation Process: Tokens are typically created through token generation events, which may include initial coin offerings (ICOs), token sales, airdrops, or mining processes.

Initial Distribution Mechanisms: Different projects employ various methods to distribute tokens initially, aiming for broad participation and fair allocation among stakeholders.

Importance of Fair Distribution: Fair token distribution is crucial for maintaining decentralization and preventing concentration of power among a small group of holders, which could lead to network manipulation or centralization risks.

Tokenomics Considerations: Tokenomics models should consider factors like inflationary vs. deflationary supply dynamics, token emission schedules, vesting periods, and mechanisms to incentivize long-term participation and contribution to the ecosystem.

2. Token Utility and Value Proposition:

Token utility refers to the practical uses and benefits that tokens offer within a blockchain ecosystem. Key points include:

Driving Demand and Adoption: Tokens with clear utility drive demand as users seek access to platform features, services, or incentives.

Value Proposition: Establishing a clear value proposition is essential for tokens to differentiate themselves and attract users, investors, and developers to the ecosystem.

Examples of Token Utility: Utility tokens can be used for accessing platform functionalities (e.g., paying transaction fees, accessing premium features), participating in governance processes, earning rewards, or representing ownership rights to digital or physical assets.

3. Token Economics Models:

Token economics models govern how tokens are distributed, circulated, and valued within a blockchain ecosystem. Key points include:

Consensus Mechanisms: Different consensus mechanisms (e.g.,

proof-of-work, proof-of-stake, delegated proof-of-stake) impact token economics by influencing token issuance, security, and network participation.

Token Velocity: Token velocity measures the rate at which tokens are exchanged within the ecosystem and affects their value. Lower velocity tokens tend to have higher values as they are held for longer periods.

Scarcity and Demand: Scarcity, driven by limited token supply or deflationary mechanisms, can increase demand and value perception among users and investors.

Network Effects: Strong network effects, characterized by growing user adoption and ecosystem activity, contribute to increased token demand and value over time.

This chapter provides readers with a comprehensive understanding of tokenomics fundamentals, including token supply dynamics, utility, and value proposition, as well as different token economic models. Feel free to expand on specific examples, case studies, or technical aspects to enrich the discussion and provide practical insights into the world of Tokenomics.

CHAPTER FIVE: TOKEN LAUNCH MECHANISMS

1. Initial Coin Offerings (ICOs):

Define ICOs as a fundraising mechanism where new cryptocurrency projects sell their native tokens to early investors in exchange for funding.

Discuss the evolution of ICOs, from their early days characterized by high levels of speculation and regulatory uncertainty to more regulated and compliant fundraising methods.

Explore the process of conducting an ICO, including token issuance, token sale structures, fundraising goals, and regulatory compliance considerations.

Highlight successful ICO projects and examine their impact on the cryptocurrency ecosystem.

2. Security Token Offerings (STOs):

Define STOs as tokenized offerings that represent ownership in real-world assets or securities and are subject to securities regulations.

Differentiate STOs from traditional ICOs by their compliance with securities laws, investor protections, and asset-backed nature.

Discuss the benefits of STOs, including increased transparency, regulatory compliance, and broader investor access to traditional assets.

Explore the challenges and regulatory considerations associated with launching STOs, including registration requirements, investor accreditation, and compliance with securities laws.

3. Initial Decentralized Exchange Offerings (IDOs):

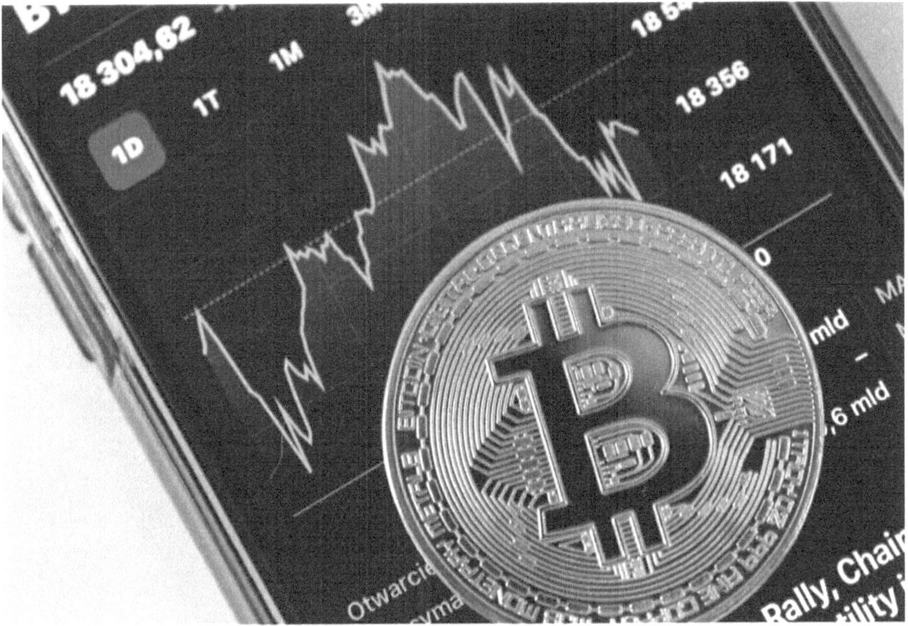

Define IDOs as token sales conducted directly on decentralized exchanges (DEXs), where projects distribute tokens to liquidity providers and decentralized exchange users.

Discuss the advantages of IDOs, including censorship resistance, reduced reliance on centralized intermediaries, and broader market access.

Explore the risks and challenges associated with IDOs, including liquidity constraints, market manipulation, and regulatory uncertainties.

Highlight successful IDO platforms and projects and examine their impact on decentralized finance (DeFi) and token distribution models.

4. Initial Exchange Offerings (IEOs):

Define IEOs as token sales conducted on centralized cryptocurrency exchanges, where the exchange acts as a trusted intermediary to facilitate token issuance, fundraising, and investor protection.

Discuss the benefits of IEOs, including enhanced investor trust, liquidity provision, and marketing support from exchange platforms.

Explore the criteria and requirements for launching IEOs on cryptocurrency exchanges, including due diligence processes, listing fees, and compliance checks.

Examine successful IEO projects and evaluate the effectiveness of IEOs as a fundraising mechanism in the cryptocurrency market.

Chapter Five: Token Launch Mechanisms

1. Initial Coin Offerings (ICOs):

Definition and Evolution: Understanding ICOs as a fundraising mechanism where new cryptocurrency projects sell their native tokens to early investors.

Process and Structure: Exploring the process of conducting an

ICO, including token issuance, sale structures, fundraising goals, and investor participation.

Regulatory Considerations: Discussing the regulatory landscape surrounding ICOs, including compliance with securities laws, investor protection measures, and regulatory enforcement actions.

Success Stories and Impact: Highlighting successful ICO projects and their impact on the cryptocurrency ecosystem, including notable case studies and lessons learned.

2. Security Token Offerings (STOs):

Definition and Characteristics: Defining STOs as tokenized offerings that represent ownership in real-world assets or securities, subject to securities regulations.

Differences from ICOs: Contrasting STOs with traditional ICOs in terms of compliance, investor protections, asset-backed nature, and regulatory considerations.

Benefits and Challenges: Exploring the benefits of STOs, such as increased transparency, regulatory compliance, and broader investor access, along with challenges like regulatory complexities and compliance costs.

Regulatory Compliance: Discussing the regulatory requirements and compliance considerations associated with launching STOs, including registration, investor accreditation, and compliance with securities laws.

3. Initial Decentralized Exchange Offerings (IDOs):

Definition and Process: Defining IDOs as token sales conducted directly on decentralized exchanges (DEXs), offering advantages such as censorship resistance and broader market access.

Advantages and Risks: Exploring the advantages of IDOs, including reduced reliance on centralized intermediaries, as well as risks such as liquidity constraints, market manipulation, and regulatory uncertainties.

Platform and Project Examples: Highlighting successful IDO platforms and projects, evaluating their impact on decentralized finance (DeFi), and examining their token distribution models.

4. Initial Exchange Offerings (IEOs):

Definition and Functionality: Defining IEOs as token sales conducted on centralized cryptocurrency exchanges, where the exchange acts as a trusted intermediary to facilitate token issuance, fundraising, and investor protection.

Benefits and Criteria: Discussing the benefits of IEOs, including enhanced investor trust, liquidity provision, and marketing support from exchange platforms, along with the criteria and requirements for launching IEOs.

Case Studies and Effectiveness: Examining successful IEO projects and evaluating the effectiveness of IEOs as a fundraising mechanism in the cryptocurrency market, including notable examples and outcomes.

This chapter provides readers with a comprehensive overview of various token launch mechanisms, including ICOs, STOs, IDOs, and IEOs. It explores the advantages, challenges, and regulatory considerations associated with each fundraising method, as well as the evolving landscape of token sales in the cryptocurrency market.

CHAPTER SIX: USE CASES OF TOKENS

1. Decentralized Finance (DeFi):

Define DeFi and its role in reshaping traditional financial services using blockchain technology and smart contracts.

Explore various DeFi applications powered by tokens, including decentralized exchanges (DEXs), lending platforms, liquidity pools, yield farming, and synthetic assets.

Discuss the benefits of DeFi, such as accessibility, transparency, composability, and financial inclusion, enabled by tokenized protocols and permissionless innovation.

2. Non-Fungible Tokens (NFTs):

Discuss the emergence of NFTs as a revolutionary technology for tokenizing and trading unique digital assets, such as digital art, collectibles, gaming items, and virtual real estate.

Explore the diverse use cases of NFTs across industries, including digital art marketplaces, gaming ecosystems, intellectual property rights management, and content monetization.

Highlight the transformative impact of NFTs on creative expression, ownership rights, and the democratization of digital content creation and distribution.

3. Gaming and Virtual Assets:

Examine the integration of tokens and blockchain technology in the gaming industry, enabling ownership, interoperability, and scarcity of in-game assets.

Discuss the use of gaming tokens for in-game purchases, rewards, asset trading, digital identity, and decentralized governance within gaming ecosystems.

Explore the potential of blockchain-based gaming platforms to disrupt traditional gaming models, foster player-driven economies, and enhance player experiences.

4. Supply Chain Management:

Explore the application of tokens in supply chain management, enabling transparent, traceable, and efficient tracking of goods and transactions across the supply chain.

Discuss how supply chain tokens facilitate real-time visibility, provenance verification, compliance management, and stakeholder collaboration in global supply chains.

Highlight use cases of supply chain tokens in industries such as agriculture, logistics, manufacturing, and retail, addressing challenges related to counterfeit goods, product recalls, and sustainability.

5. Identity Verification and Digital Rights Management:

Discuss the use of tokens for identity verification, authentication, and access control in digital ecosystems, ensuring privacy, security, and user sovereignty.

Explore token-based solutions for managing digital rights, licensing agreements, and intellectual property protection in media, entertainment, publishing, and content distribution industries.

Highlight innovative projects leveraging tokens to empower individuals, artists, and content creators with control over their personal data and creative works.

This chapter provides readers with insights into the diverse use cases of tokens across various industries and applications, including decentralized finance, non-fungible tokens, gaming, supply chain management, and digital rights management.

CHAPTER SIX: USE CASES OF TOKENS

1. Decentralized Finance (DeFi):

Definition and Overview: Understanding DeFi as the application of blockchain technology and smart contracts to recreate traditional financial services in a decentralized and permissionless manner.

Tokenized Protocols: Exploring various DeFi protocols powered by tokens, including decentralized exchanges (DEXs), lending platforms, liquidity pools, yield farming, and synthetic assets.

Benefits of DeFi: Discussing the benefits of DeFi, such as accessibility, transparency, composability, and financial inclusion, enabled by tokenized protocols and permissionless innovation.

Case Studies and Examples: Highlighting successful DeFi projects and their impact on the financial landscape, including notable platforms, governance models, and emerging trends.

2. Non-Fungible Tokens (NFTs):

Introduction to NFTs: Defining NFTs as unique digital assets that represent ownership or proof of authenticity of specific items or content on the blockchain.

Diverse Use Cases: Exploring the diverse applications of NFTs across industries, including digital art marketplaces, gaming ecosystems, intellectual property rights management, and content monetization.

Transformative Impact: Discussing the transformative impact of NFTs on creative expression, ownership rights, and the democratization of digital content creation and distribution.

Emerging Trends: Highlighting emerging trends and innovations in the NFT space, including cross-platform interoperability, fractional ownership, and tokenized real-world assets.

3. Gaming and Virtual Assets:

Tokenization in Gaming: Examining the integration of tokens and blockchain technology in the gaming industry, enabling ownership, interoperability, and scarcity of in-game assets.

Use Cases of Gaming Tokens: Discussing the use of gaming tokens for in-game purchases, rewards, asset trading, digital identity, and decentralized governance within gaming ecosystems.

Disruptive Potential: Exploring the potential of blockchain-based gaming platforms to disrupt traditional gaming models, foster player-driven economies, and enhance player experiences.

Case Studies and Examples: Highlighting successful blockchain-based gaming projects and their impact on the gaming industry, including popular games, virtual economies, and player communities.

4. Supply Chain Management:

Tokenization in Supply Chain: Exploring the application of tokens in supply chain management, enabling transparent, traceable, and efficient tracking of goods and transactions.

Benefits of Supply Chain Tokens: Discussing how supply chain tokens facilitate real-time visibility, provenance verification, compliance management, and stakeholder collaboration in global supply chains.

Industry Applications: Highlighting use cases of supply chain tokens in industries such as agriculture, logistics, manufacturing, and retail, addressing challenges related to counterfeit goods, product recalls, and sustainability.

Adoption Challenges: Discussing challenges and barriers to the adoption of tokenized supply chain solutions, including interoperability, data privacy, and regulatory compliance.

5. Identity Verification and Digital Rights Management:

Tokenized Identity Solutions: Exploring the use of tokens for identity verification, authentication, and access control in digital ecosystems, ensuring privacy, security, and user sovereignty.

Digital Rights Management: Discussing token-based solutions for managing digital rights, licensing agreements, and intellectual property protection in media, entertainment, publishing, and content distribution industries.

Empowering Individuals: Highlighting innovative projects leveraging tokens to empower individuals, artists, and content creators with control over their personal data and creative works.

Regulatory Considerations: Discussing regulatory considerations and challenges associated with tokenized identity and digital rights management solutions, including data protection, copyright enforcement, and consumer rights.

This chapter provides readers with a comprehensive exploration of the diverse use cases of tokens across various industries and applications. It covers decentralized finance, non-fungible tokens, gaming, supply chain management, and digital rights management, highlighting examples, case studies, and emerging trends in each domain.

CHAPTER SEVEN: TOKEN INVESTMENT STRATEGIES

1. Fundamental Analysis of Token Projects:

Importance of Fundamental Analysis: Discussing the significance of fundamental analysis in evaluating the long-term viability and potential of token projects.

Key Metrics and Factors: Exploring essential factors to consider during fundamental analysis, such as project whitepapers, team expertise, technology stack, community engagement, and roadmap execution.

Assessment Criteria: Highlighting the importance of assessing problem-solving capacity, market fit, competitive landscape, and regulatory compliance of token projects.

Case Studies: Providing examples and case studies of successful fundamental analysis approaches in identifying promising token investments.

2. Technical Analysis and Market Sentiment:

Understanding Technical Analysis: Defining technical analysis and its role in understanding price trends, market behavior, and investor sentiment in token markets.

Common Analysis Tools: Exploring common technical analysis tools and indicators used to analyze token price movements, including moving averages, relative strength index (RSI), and Fibonacci retracements.

Monitoring Market Dynamics: Discussing the importance of monitoring trading volumes, order book depth, liquidity levels, and market sentiment indicators to identify trading opportunities and market trends.

Sentiment Analysis: Providing insights into sentiment analysis techniques, sentiment indicators, and sentiment-driven market dynamics affecting token prices.

3. Risk Management and Portfolio Diversification:

Importance of Risk Management: Highlighting the importance of risk management strategies in token investment portfolios to mitigate downside risks and preserve capital.

Diversification Principles: Discussing portfolio diversification principles, including asset allocation, risk tolerance assessment, and investment horizon considerations.

Risk Management Techniques: Exploring risk management techniques such as position sizing, stop-loss orders, profit-taking strategies, and portfolio rebalancing to manage exposure to market volatility and unforeseen events.

Constructing Resilient Portfolios: Providing practical tips and guidelines for constructing resilient token investment portfolios tailored to investors' risk profiles and investment objectives.

This chapter provides readers with insights into effective token investment strategies, including fundamental analysis, technical analysis, market sentiment analysis, risk management, and portfolio diversification. It covers essential principles and techniques for evaluating token projects, analyzing market dynamics, and managing investment risks in the Cryptocurrency market.

CHAPTER EIGHT: TOKEN SECURITY AND BEST PRACTICES

1. Smart Contract Audits:

Definition and Importance: Discussing the importance of smart contract audits in ensuring the security, reliability, and functionality of blockchain-based applications.

Audit Process: Explaining the process of smart contract audits, including code review, vulnerability assessment, and penetration testing conducted by professional audit firms.

Best Practices: Highlighting the significance of conducting multiple audits and implementing best practices in smart contract development to mitigate potential risks and vulnerabilities.

Common Vulnerabilities: Providing insights into common smart contract vulnerabilities and attack vectors, such as reentrancy, integer overflow, and authorization flaws, along with strategies to address them.

2. Wallet Security and Cold Storage:

Importance of Wallet Security: Exploring the importance of

wallet security in safeguarding cryptocurrency assets against theft, loss, and unauthorized access.

Best Practices: Discussing best practices for securing cryptocurrency wallets, including the use of hardware wallets, multi-signature wallets, and encrypted storage solutions.

Cold Storage: Highlighting the concept of cold storage as a secure method for storing cryptocurrency assets offline, away from internet-connected devices and potential hacking threats.

Guidance and Recommendations: Providing guidance on choosing reputable wallet providers, setting up strong passwords, enabling two-factor authentication (2FA), and practicing safe storage practices to enhance wallet security.

3. Avoiding Scams and Fraudulent Projects:

Understanding Scams: Educating readers about common scams and fraudulent schemes prevalent in the cryptocurrency space, such as Ponzi schemes, pump-and-dump schemes, and fake ICOs.

Red Flags and Warning Signs: Discussing red flags and warning signs of fraudulent projects, including unrealistic promises of high returns, anonymous teams, lack of transparency, and pressure tactics.

Due Diligence and Research: Providing tips and strategies for conducting due diligence and research before investing in token projects, including verifying team credentials, analyzing project whitepapers, and assessing community feedback.

Empowerment and Protection: Empowering readers with knowledge and resources to protect themselves against scams, fraud, and phishing attacks in the cryptocurrency ecosystem.

This chapter provides readers with insights into token security best practices, including smart contract audits, wallet security, cold storage, and avoiding scams and fraudulent projects. It covers essential principles and techniques for ensuring the security and integrity of token investments and minimizing the risks associated with cryptocurrency ownership.

CHAPTER NINE: EMERGING TRENDS IN TOKENIZATION

1. Decentralized Autonomous Organizations (DAOs):

Understanding DAOs: Decentralized Autonomous Organizations (DAOs) are entities governed by smart contracts and run by code rather than centralized control. They enable decentralized decision-making and governance through blockchain technology.

Principles of DAOs: DAOs operate on principles of transparency, accountability, and community-driven participation. They allow members to vote on proposals, allocate funds, and manage organizational resources without relying on centralized authorities.

Real-World Examples: DAOs have various applications, including governance tokens in decentralized finance (DeFi), community-driven projects, and decentralized governance of protocols and platforms.

Opportunities and Challenges: While DAOs offer opportunities for decentralized decision-making and community empowerment, challenges include regulatory compliance, governance mechanisms, and scalability issues that need to be addressed for widespread adoption.

2. Tokenized Assets (Real Estate, Art, Securities):

Concept of Tokenized Assets: Tokenized assets represent ownership or shares of traditional assets like real estate, art, and securities on blockchain platforms. They enable fractional ownership, liquidity provision, and global market access for investors.

Benefits of Tokenization: Tokenizing assets democratizes access to traditionally illiquid assets, opening up investment opportunities to a broader audience. It enhances liquidity, reduces transaction costs, and facilitates faster settlement.

Real-World Examples: Examples of tokenized assets include platforms for tokenized real estate, art marketplaces, and security token offerings (STOs) that enable investors to access traditional asset classes in a digital format.

Regulatory Considerations: Tokenized assets face regulatory considerations and legal frameworks that vary across jurisdictions. Compliance with securities regulations, investor protections, and custody solutions are crucial aspects to consider in tokenized asset investments.

3. Cross-Chain Interoperability and Scalability Solutions:

Interoperability and Scalability: Cross-chain interoperability and scalability solutions are essential for achieving seamless communication and scalability across diverse blockchain networks.

Interoperability Protocols: Protocols like atomic swaps, sidechains, and interoperability bridges facilitate asset transfer, data sharing, and smart contract execution between different blockchain platforms.

Scalability Solutions: Layer 2 solutions, sharding, and blockchain interoperability frameworks address scalability challenges by enabling faster transaction processing and higher throughput.

Importance in Blockchain Ecosystem: Interoperability and

scalability solutions foster innovation, interoperability between blockchain networks, and scalability for decentralized applications (dApps), enables broader adoption and use cases across various industries.

This chapter provides readers with a comprehensive overview of emerging trends in tokenization, including Decentralized Autonomous Organizations (DAOs), tokenized assets, and cross-chain interoperability solutions. It covers fundamental principles, real-world examples, opportunities, and challenges associated with these trends, offering insights into the evolving landscape of tokenization in the blockchain industry.

CHAPTER TEN: CONCLUSION AND FUTURE OUTLOOK

1. Summary of Key Concepts:

In this final chapter, we reflect on the journey through the world of tokenomics explored in this book. We revisit the fundamental principles discussed, ranging from tokenomics basics to advanced investment strategies and security practices. Key takeaways are summarized, emphasizing the transformative potential of tokenization across various industries and sectors.

2. Reflections on the Future of Tokenomics:

As we gaze into the horizon of the token economy, we contemplate the dynamic nature of tokenomics and its profound impact on the future. Emerging trends such as decentralized finance (DeFi), non-fungible tokens (NFTs), decentralized autonomous organizations (DAOs), and cross-chain interoperability solutions are examined. Speculative insights are offered regarding potential developments, challenges, and opportunities that lie ahead in the ever-evolving landscape of tokenomics.